A Treasury of Christian Verse

A
Treasury of
Christian Verse

Selected and edited by
HUGH MARTIN

FORTRESS PRESS · PHILADELPHIA

© SCM Press Ltd 1959

Printed in Great Britain

CONTENTS

[5]

[6]

[7]

[8]

[9]

INTRODUCTION

This is not one more anthology of religious verse in general. It is concerned with Jesus Christ Himself, as reflected in English verse through the centuries, from the first beginnings of our poetry to the present day. Many of the greatest names in the roll are represented, though some appear to have said nothing in their published works on this theme. Several of the writers are little known to the general reader. Not all speak from an orthodox Christian standpoint: some indeed asserted, regretfully or defiantly, that they were unbelievers. One or two of the entries would probably have been excluded on strictly literary standards, but, like the verse from John Bunyan, deserved their place on other grounds. Familiar hymns have been deliberately omitted, though two or three of these poems may be found, usually in amended form, in a hymn book.

Much might have been written by way of commentary on both writers and verses, but it seemed best to let them tell their own story. Notes have been confined to explanations of archaic or dialect words.

HUGH MARTIN

ACKNOWLEDGEMENTS

Our grateful thanks are due to the following for permission to use copyright material:

The Clarendon Press for *Noel: Christmas Eve, 1913* by Robert Bridges;

Burns & Oates Ltd for *No Sudden Thing* and *He Rose Again* by Alice Meynell;

Sidgwick & Jackson Ltd for *The Lamb of God* by Katherine Tynan Hinkson and fifteen lines from *Little Plays of St Francis* by Laurence Housman;

Jonathan Cape Ltd for *A Prayer for the Healing of the Wounds of Christ* by Laurence Housman;

A. D. Peters & Co. for *Our Lord and Our Lady* by Hilaire Belloc (from his *Sonnets and Verse*);

The Talbot Press Ltd, Dublin for *I Saw His Blood upon the Rose* by Joseph Mary Plunkett;

The Macmillan Co. for thirty-six lines from *The Everlasting Mercy* (reprinted with permission from *Poems* by John Masefield, copyright 1912 by The Macmillan Co., renewed 1940 by John Masefield);

Rupert Hart-Davis Ltd for seventeen lines from *Nicodemus* by Andrew Young;

Harcourt, Brace & World, Inc. for sixteen lines from *The Rock* by T. S. Eliot (copyright, 1934, by Harcourt, Brace & World, Inc.; copyright, 1962, by T. S. Eliot; reprinted by permission of the publishers);

the family of the late Mr H. C. Bradby for *Night Thoughts*;

John Murray (Publishers) Ltd and Houghton Mifflin Co. for *Christmas* by John Betjeman (from his *Collected Poems*).

The Editor of this volume and the Publishers have endeavoured to trace copyrights, but present their apologies if any have been unwittingly infringed.

[13]

CHRIST THE CORNERSTONE

O King! Thou art the wall-stone,
which of old the workmen
from their work rejected!
Well it Thee beseemeth
that Thou hold the headship
of this Hall of glory,
and should'st join together
with a fastening firm
the broad-spaced walls
of the flint unbreakable
all fitly framed together;
that among earth's dwellers
all with sight of eyes
may for ever wonder.
O Prince of glory!
now through skill and wisdom
manifest Thy handiwork,
true-fast and firm-set
in sovran splendour.

Cynewulf. Based upon the antiphon O REX GENTIUM

CHRIST THE VICTOR

Lo, the holy Hero-warrior, King of glory,
He the Helm of Heaven, hath arrayed the war
Right against His ancient foes, with His only might.
. . . . . .
Now will He seek the spirit's throne of grace,
He, the Saviour of souls, the proper bairn of God,
After His war-play! Forward now, ye comrades,
Frankly march along! Open, O ye gates!
He will into you. He, of all the wielder,—
He, the City's King—He, creation's Lord,
Now His folk will lead, reft from the devils,
To the joy of joys, by His own victory.
'Twixt God and man He places a ghostly pledge
Of love—life's solace and of all light joy.

From *Cynewulf's* CHRIST. Probably 8th century.

(The section on the Ascension, in which he sees the host of angels
coming to meet the ascending Christ.)

Both quotations from Cynewulf are taken from the modernized version
in *The Christ of English Poetry*, C. W. Stubbs.

A PRAYER TO JESUS

Jhesu, since thou me made and bought,
Thou be my love and all my thought,
And help that I may to Thee be brought;
Withouten Thee I may do nought.

Jhesu, since Thou must do Thy will,
And naething is that Thee may let;
With Thy grace my heart fulfill,
My love and my liking in Thee set.

Jhesu, at Thy will
I pray that I might be;
All my heart fulfill
With perfect love to Thee.

That I have done ill,
Jhesu, forgive Thou me;
And suffer me never to spill,
Jhesu, for pity. Amen.

Richard Rolle, 1290-1349

let: forbid, stop; at: in accordance with; spill: perish.

CHRIST'S COMPLAINT

Unkind man, give heed to me
And see what pain I suffer for thee.

Sinful man, on thee I cry,
Solely for thy love I die.

Behold the blood from me down rins,
Not for my guilt but for thy sins.

My hands, my feet, with nails are fast,
Sinews and veins entirely burst.

The blood from out my heart-root,
Look! it falls down to my foot.

Of all the pain that I suffer sair,
Within my heart it grieves me mair

The unkindness that I find in thee,
Who for thy love, thus hanged on tree.

Alas! Why lovest thou me nought,
And I thy love so dear have bought?

Save thou me love, thou dost me wrong,
Since I have loved thee so long.

Two and thirty year and mair
I was for thee in travail sair;

With hunger, thirst, heat and cold,
For thy love hath bought and sold.

Pinëd, nailed, and done on tree,
All, man, for love of thee.

Love thou me, as thou well ought,
And from sin thee withdraw;

I give thee my body, with wounds sair,
And thereto shall I give thee mair

Above all this certain, Iwis;
On earth my grace, in heaven my bliss.   JHESU.

Richard Rolle

Based on the Latin of Philippe de Grève, Chancellor of Paris, d. 1236, Rolles' version has been somewhat modernized.

Iwis: truly.

[19]

LOVE UNFEIGNED

O yonge fresshe folkes, he or she,
In which ay love up-groweth with your age,
Repeireth hom from worldly vanite!
And of your herte up-casteth the visage
To thilke God that after His image
You made; and thinketh al n'is but a fayre
This world, that passeth sone as floures faire!

And loveth Him, the which that right for love
Upon a cross, our soules for to beye,
First starf, and roos, and sit in hevene above;
For He n'ill falsen no wight, dar I seye,
That wol his herte al hoolly on Him leye!
And sin He best to love is, and most meke,
What nedeth feyned loves for to seke?

Geoffrey Chaucer, 1340?-1400,
from TROILUS AND CRISEYDE

Repeireth: repair ye, and so with up-casteth, thinketh, loveth; sone:
soon; beye: buy; starf: died; falsen: betray; hoolly: wholly; sin: since.

LIKE A LAMB OFFERED IN SACRIFICE

Behold My love, and give Me thine again,
  Behold I died Thy ransom for to pay;
See how My heart is open broad and plain,
  Thy ghostly enemies only to affray;
An harder battle no man might essay,
  Of all triumphs the greatest high emprise;
Wherefore, O man, no longer thee dismay,
  I gave My blood for thee in sacrifice.

Turn home again; thy sin do thou forsake,
  Behold and see if ought be left behind,
How I to mercy am ready thee to take.
  Give Me thy heart, and be no more unkind;
My love and thine, together do them bind,
  And let them never part in no wise.
When Thou wert lost, thy soul again to find
  My blood I offered for thee in sacrifice.

Tarry no longer! Toward thine heritage
  Haste on thy way, and be of right good cheer.
Go each day onward on thy pilgrimage,
  Think how short time thou shalt abide here.
Thy place is bigged above the starres clear,
  None earthly palace wrought in so stately wise.
Come on, my friend, my brother most entire.
  For thee I offered My blood in sacrifice.

John Lydgate, 1370-1451

Bigged: builded.

THE BABE FORESEES THE CROSS

So blessed a sight it was to see
How Mary rocked her Son so free,
So fair she rocked, and sang: 'by, by,'
Mine own dear moder, sing lulley.
    Lulley, Jhesu, lulley, lulley.
    Mine own dear moder, sing lulley!

'Mine own dear son, why weepest thou thus?
Is not thy fader king of bliss?
Have I not done that in me is?
Your grievance, tell me what it is!'

'Therefore, moder, weep I nought,
But for the woe that shall be wrought
To me, or I mankind have bought.
Mine own dear moder, sing lulley!

Moder, the time ye shall see,
Sorrow shall break your heart in three,
So foul the Jews shall fare with me.
Mine own dear moder, sing lulley!

When I am nakid they will me take
And fast bind me to a stake,
And beat me sore for mannis sake.
Mine own dear moder, sing lulley!

Upon the cross they shall me cast,
Hand and foot nail me fast.
Yet gall shall be my drink at last;
Thus shall my life be passed away.

Ah! dear moder, yet shall a spear
My heart in sunder all to-tear,
No wonder though I care-full were.
Mine own dear moder, sing lulley!

[22]

Now, dear moder, sing lulley,
Put away all heaviness,
Into this world I took the way,
Again to heaven I shall me dress.
   There joy is without end, ay,
    Mine own dear moder, sing lulley!

From a 14th century MS in Balliol College, Oxford

Dress: direct my way.

CHRIST'S LOVE-SONG TO MAN

Love me brought
And love me wrought,
Man, to be thy fere;
Love me fed,
And love me led,
And love me letteth here.

Love me slew,
And love me drew,
And love me laid on bier;
Love is my peace,
For love I chese
Man to buyen dear.

Ne dread thee nought,
I have thee sought
Both by day and night,
To haven thee;
Well is to me,
I have thee won in fight.

From a MS (? 14th century) in the National
Library of Scotland

fere: companion, friend; letteth: ? keeps, retains; chese: chose.

LOVE TRUE AND EVER GREEN

All other love is like the moon
That waxeth or waneth as flower in plain,
As flower that blooms and fadeth soon,
As day that showereth and ends in rain.

All other love begins with bliss,
In weeping and woe makes its ending;
No love there is that's our whole bliss
But that which rests on heaven's king.

Whose love is true and ever green,
And ever full without waning;
His love sweetens without teen,
His love is endless and a-ring.

All other love I fly for thee,
Tell me, tell me where thou liest!
'In Marie, mild and free,
I shall be found, but more in Crist.'

Crist me found, not I thee hast,
Hold me to thee with all thy main;
Help yield that my love be steadfast,
Lest thus soon it turn again.

Now when still my heart is sore,
Iwis they spilt mine hearte-blood;
God knows my love; I care no more—
Yet I hope his will be good.

Alas! what will I at Rome?
Speak I may in lore of love.
Undone I am by mannis doom,
Save He me help that sits above.

c. 1350

teen : sorrow; a-ring : perfect; Iwis : truly; lore : teaching.

[25]

ON THE NATIVITY OF CHRIST

Rorate coeli desuper!
　　Hevins, distil your balmy schouris!
For now is risen the bricht day-ster,
　　Fro the rose Mary, flour of flouris:
　　The cleir Sone, quhom no cloud devouris,
Surmounting Phebus in the Est,
　　Is cumin of his hevinly touris:—
　　　　Et nobis Puer natus est.

Archangellis, angellis and dompnationis,
　　Tronis, potestatis and marteiris seir,
And all ye hevinly operationis,
Ster, planeit, firmament, and spheir,
　　Fire, erd, air and water cleir,
To Him gife loving, most and lest,
　　That come in to so meik maneir;
　　　　Et nobis Puer natus est.

Synnaris be glad, and penance do,
　　And thank your Maker hairtfully;
For He that ye micht nocht come to
　　To you is cumin full humbly
　　Your soulis with His blood to buy
And loose you of the fiendis arrest—
　　And only of His own mercy;
　　　　Pro nobis Puer natus est.

All clergy do to Him inclyne,
　　And bow unto that Bairn benyng,
And do your observance divyne
　　To Him that is of kingis King:
　　Encense His altar, read and sing
In holy kirk, with mind degest,
　　Him honouring attour all thing
　　　　Qui nobis Puer natus est.

Celestial foulis in the air,
    Sing with your nottis upon hicht,
In firthis and in forrestis fair
    Be myrthful now at all your micht;
    For passit is your dully nicht,
Aurora has the cloudis perst,
        The Sone is risen with glaidsum licht,
            Et nobis Puer natus est.

Now spring up flouris fra the rute,
    Revert you upward naturaly,
In honour of the blissid frute
    That raiss up fro the rose Mary;
    Lay out your levis lustily,
Fro deid take life now at the lest
        In wirschip of that Prince worthy
            Qui nobis Puer natus est.

Sing, hevin imperial, most of hicht!
Regions of air mak armony!
All fish in flud and fowl of flicht
    Be mirthful and mak melody!
    All Gloria in excelsis cry!
Heaven, erd, se, man, bird and best,—
        He that is crownit above the sky
            Pro nobis Puer natus est!

William Dunbar, 1465-1520

Rorate, etc.: the next line is a good translation! Schouris: showers; seir:
various; erd: earth; lest: least; synnaris: sinners; benyng: benign; degest:
composed, grave; attour: above; perst: pierced; raiss: rose; levis: leaves;
best: beast; et nobis Puer natus est: 'For unto us a Boy is born.'

AN EVENING PRAYER

Jesus Lord, well of all goodness,
    For Thy great pity I Thee pray:
Forgive me all my wickedness
    Wherewith I have grieved Thee today.

Honour and praising to Thee be,
    And thanking for Thy gifts all
That I this day received of Thee;
    Now, courteous Christ, to Thee I call.

This night from peril Thou me keep,
    My bodily rest while that I take;
And as long as mine eyen sleep
    My heart in Thy service wake.

From feryng of the fiend our foe,
    From foul dreams and fantasies,
Keep this night; from sins also
    In cleanness that I may up-rise.

Save my good-doers from grievance,
    And quit them that they on me spend;
Keep my enemies from noyans
    And give them grace for to amend.

Mercy, Jesu, and grant mercy.
    My body, my soul, I Thee be-kene
In nomine patris et filii
    Et spiritus sancti.   Amen.

From RELIGIOUS LYRICS OF THE FIFTEENTH CENTURY
Edited by Carleton Brown

The spelling has been modernized. Feryng: ? peril; grievance: cause for grief; noyans: ? doing harm; be-kene: commend.

CRUCIFY HIM!

Frail multitude, whose giddy law is list,
  And best applause is windy flattering;
Most like the breath of which it doth consist,
No sooner blown but as soon vanishing,
As much desired as little profiting;
   That makes the men that have it oft as light
   As those that give it; which the proud invite,
And fear: the bad man's friend, the good man's hypocrite.

It was but now their sounding clamours sung,
  'Blessed is he that comes from the Most High.'
And all the mountains with Hosanna rung;
And now, 'Away with him—away!' they cry,
And nothing can be heard but 'Crucify!'
   It was but now the crown itself they gave,
   And golden name of King unto him gave;
And now, no king but only Caesar they will have.

It was but now they gathered blooming may,
  And of his arms disrobed the branching tree,
To strow with boughs and blossoms all thy way;
And now, the branchless trunk a cross for thee,
And may, dis-mayed, thy coronet must be.
   It was but now they were so kind to throw
   Their own best garments where thy feet should go,
And now, thyself they strip, and bleeding wounds they show.

Giles Fletcher, 1549-1611

HIS PILGRIMAGE

Give me my scallop-shell of quiet,
My staff of faith to walk upon;
My scrip of joy, immortal diet,
My bottle of salvation;
My gown of glory (hope's true gage),
And thus I'll take my pilgrimage.
Blood must be my body's only balmer,
Whilst my soul, like a quiet palmer,
Travelleth towards the land of heaven;
No other balm will there be given.
O'er the silver mountains
Where spring the nectar fountains,
There will I kiss
The bowl of bliss,
And drink my everlasting fill
Upon every milken hill.
My soul will be a-dry before,
But after it will thirst no more.

* * * *

From thence to heaven's bribeless hall,
Where no corrupted voices brawl,
No conscience molten into gold,
No forged accuser bought or sold,
No cause deferred, no vain-spent journey;
For there Christ is the King's attorney,
Who pleads for all without degrees,
And he hath angels, but no fees.
And when the twelve grand million jury
Of our sins with direful fury
'Gainst our souls black verdicts give,
Christ pleads His death, and then we live.

Sir Walter Raleigh, 1552-1618

Angels: a punning reference to the gold coin of his day.

[30]

EASTER MORNING

Most glorious Lord of life, that on this day
Didst make Thy triumph over death and sin,
And having harrowed hell didst bring again
Captivity thence captive, us to win;
This joyous day, dear Lord, with joy begin,
And grant that we, for whom Thou diddest die,
Being with Thy dear blood clean washed from sin,
May live for ever in felicity;
And that Thy love we weighing worthily,
May likewise love Thee for the same again;
And for Thy sake that all like dear didst buy,
With love may one another entertain.
So let us love, dear love, like as we ought;
Love is the lesson which the Lord us taught.

Edmund Spenser, 1552-99

HYMN OF HEAVENLY LOVE

Out of the bosom of eternal bliss,
In which He reignèd with his Glorious Sire,
He down descended, like a most demiss
And abject thrall, in flesh's frail attire,
That He for man might pay sin's deadly hire,
And him restore unto that happy state
In which he stood before his hapless fate.
O blessèd Well of love! O Flower of grace!
O glorious Morning Star! O Lamp of light!
Most lively Image of Thy Father's face,
Eternal King of glory, Lord of might,
Meek Lamb of God, before all worlds behight,
How can we Thee requite for all this good?
Or what can prize with Thy most precious blood?
Yet nought Thou ask'st in lieu of all this love
But love of us, for guerdon of Thy pain:
Ay me! what can us less than that behove?
Had He required life for us again,
Had it been wrong to ask His own with gain?
He gave us life; He it restorèd lost;
Then life were least that us so little cost.
But He our life hath left unto us free,
Free that was thrall, and blessèd that was banned;
Ne ought demands but that we loving be,
As He Himself hath loved us aforehand,
And bound thereto with an eternal band,
His first to love that us so dearly bought,
And next our brethren, to His image wrought.

Edmund Spenser

Demiss: submissive; prize: be equal in value; ne: not.

NEW PRINCE, NEW POMP

Behold, a silly, tender Babe,
  In freezing winter night,
In homely manger trembling lies,
  Alas! a piteous sight.
The inns are full, no man will yield
  This little pilgrim bed;
But forced is He with silly beasts
  In crib to shroud His head.
Despise Him not for lying there;
  First what He is enquire;
As orient pearl is often found
  In depth of dirty mire,
Weight not His crib, His wooden dish,
  Nor beasts that by Him feed;
Weigh not His mother's poor attire,
  Nor Joseph's simple weed.
This stable is a Prince's court,
  The crib His chair of state;
The beasts are parcel of His pomp,
  The wooden dish His plate.
The persons in that poor attire
  His royal liveries wear;
This Prince Himself, is come from heaven;
  This pomp is prizèd there.
With joy approach, O Christian wight!
  Do homage to thy King;
And highly praise this humble pomp
  Which He from Heaven doth bring.

Robert Southwell, 1561?-95

Silly: innocent, helpless.

LAUD'S HIGHEST THEME

I praise Him most, I love Him best, all praise and love is
    His;
While Him I love, in Him I live, and cannot live amiss.
Love's sweetest mark, laud's highest theme, man's most
    desirèd light,
To love Him life, to leave Him death, to live in Him delight.
He mine by gift, I His by debt, thus to each other due,
First Friend He was, best Friend He is, all times will try
    Him true;
His knowledge rules, His strength defends, His love doth
    cherish all;
His birth our joy, His life our light, His death our end of
    thrall.

Robert Southwell

GOOD FRIDAY, 1613. RIDING WESTWARD

... I am carried towards the West
This day, when my soul's form bends toward the East.
There I should see a Sun, by rising set,
And by that setting endless day beget;
But that Christ on this Cross did rise and fall,
Sin had eternally benighted all.
Yet dare I almost be glad, I do not see
That spectacle of too much weight for me.
Who sees God's face, that is self life, must die;
What a death were it then to see God die?
It made His own lieutenant, Nature, shrink,
It made His footstool crack, and the sun wink.
Could I behold those hands which span the poles,
And turn all spheres at once, pierced with those holes?
Could I behold that endless height which is
Zenith to us and our antipodes,
Humbled below us? or that blood which is
The seat of all our souls, if not of His,
Made dirt of dust, or that flesh which was worn,
By God, for His apparel, rag'd and torn?
If on these things I durst not look, durst I
On His distressed Mother cast mine eye,
Who was God's partner here, and furnished thus
Half of that sacrifice which ransomed us?
Though these things, as I ride, be from mine eye,
They're present yet unto my memory,
For that looks towards them; and Thou look'st towards me,
O Saviour, as Thou hang'st upon the tree;
I turn my back to Thee but to receive
Corrections till Thy mercies bid Thee leave.
O think me worth Thine anger, punish me,
Burn off my rust, and my deformity;
Restore Thine image, so much, by Thy grace,
That Thou may'st know me, and I'll turn my face.

John Donne, 1573-1631

A HYMN ON THE NATIVITY
OF MY SAVIOUR

I sing the Birth was born to-night,
The Author both of life and light;
  The angels so did sound it,
And like the ravished shepherds said,
Who saw the light, and were afraid,
  Yet searched, and true they found it.

The Son of God, th' Eternal King,
That did us all salvation bring,
  And freed the soul from danger;
He whom the whole world could not take,
The Word, which Heaven and Earth did make,
  Was now laid in a manger.

The Father's wisdom willed it so,
The Son's obedience knew no No.
  Both wills were in one stature,
And as that wisdom had decreed,
The Word was now made Flesh indeed,
  And took on Him our nature.

What comfort by Him do we win,
Who made Himself the price of sin
  To make us heirs of glory?
To see this Babe all innocence,
A martyr born in our defence:
  Can man forget this story?

Ben Jonson, 1573-1637

HYMN WRITTEN AT THE HOLY SEPULCHRE IN JERUSALEM

Saviour of mankind, Man, Emmanuel!
Who sinless died for sin, who vanquished hell;
The first-fruits of the grave; whose life did give
Light to our darkness; in whose death we live:—
Oh! strengthen Thou my faith, convert my will,
That mine may Thine obey; protect me still,
So that the latter death may not devour
My soul, sealed with Thy seal.—So, in the hour
When Thou (whose body sanctified this tomb,
Unjustly judged), a glorious judge shall come
To judge the world with justice; by that sign
I may be known, and entertained for Thine.

George Sandys, 1577-1644

THE DIVINE WOOER

Me, Lord? Canst Thou misspend
One word, missplace one look on me?
   Call'st me Thy love, Thy friend?
Can this poor soul the object be
Of these love-glances, those life-kindling eyes?
What? I the centre of Thy arms' embraces?
   Of all Thy labour I the prize?
   Love never mocks, truth never lies.
Oh, how I quake! Hope fear, fear hope displaces.
I would but cannot hope: such wondrous love amazes.

   See, I am black as night,
See, I am darkness: dark as hell.
   Lord, Thou more fair than light:
Heaven's sun Thy shadow. Can suns dwell
With shades? 'twixt light and darkness what commerce?
'True, thou art darkness, I thy light: My ray
   Thy mists and hellish fogs shall pierce.
   With Me, black soul, with Me converse.
I make the foul December flowery May:
Turn thou thy night to Me, I'll turn thy night to day.'

   See, Lord, see I am dead,
   Tombed in myself, myself my grave:
   A drudge, so born, so bred—
   Myself even to myself a slave.
Thou, Freedom, Life; can Life and Liberty
Love bondage, death? 'Thy Freedom I, I tied
   To loose thy bonds: be bound to Me.
   My yoke shall ease, My bonds shall free.
Dead soul, thy spring of life My dying side:
There die, with Me to live: to live in thee I died.'

Phineas Fletcher, 1582-1650

THE WONDER OF THE INCARNATION

To spread the azure canopy of heaven,
And make it twinkle with those spangs of gold,
To stay the pond'rous globe of earth so even,
That it should all, and nought should it uphold;
To give strange motions to the planets seven,
Or Jove to make so meek, or Mars so bold,
To temper what is moist, dry, hot, and cold,
Of all their jars that sweet accords are given:
Lord, to Thy wisdom's nought; nought to Thy might.
But that Thou shouldst (Thy glory laid aside)
Come meanly in mortality to bide,
And die for those deserved eternal plight,
    A wonder is so far above our wit,
    That angels stand amazed to muse on it.

William Drummond, 1585-1649

A ROCKING HYMN

Sweet baby, sleep, and nothing fear;
  For whosoever thee offends
By thy protector threatened are,
  And God and angels are thy friends.
Sweet baby, then, forbear to weep;
Be still, my babe; sweet baby, sleep.

When God with us was dwelling here,
  In little babes He took delight;
Such innocents as thou, my dear,
  Are ever precious in His sight.
Sweet baby, then, forbear to weep;
Be still, my babe; sweet baby, sleep.

A little infant once was He,
  And strength in weakness then was laid
Upon his Virgin Mother's knee,
  That power to thee might be conveyed.
Sweet baby, then, forbear to weep;
Be still, my babe; sweet baby, sleep.

In this thy frailty and thy need
  He friends and helpers doth prepare,
Which thee shall cherish, clothe and feed,
  For of thy weal they tender are.
Sweet baby, then, forbear to weep;
Be still, my babe; sweet baby, sleep.

The King of kings, when He was born,
  Had not so much for outward ease;
By Him such dressings were not worn,
  Nor such-like swaddling-clothes as these.
Sweet baby, then, forbear to weep;
Be still, my babe; sweet baby, sleep.

Within a manger lodged thy Lord,
   Where oxen lay and asses fed;
Warm rooms we do to thee afford,
   An easy cradle or a bed.
Sweet baby, then, forbear to weep;
Be still, my babe; sweet baby, sleep.

    *   *   *   *   *

Thou hast yet more to perfect this,
   A promise and an earnest got
Of gaining everlasting bliss,
   Though thou, my babe, perceiv'st it not.
Sweet baby, then, forbear to weep;
Be still, my babe; sweet baby, sleep.

George Wither, 1588-1667

MY WAY, MY LIFE, MY LIGHT

' Wherefore hidest Thou Thy face?' Job 13.24.

Why dost Thou shade Thy lovely face? O why
Does that eclipsing hand so long deny
The sunshine of Thy soul-enlivening eye?

Without that Light, what light remains in me?
Thou art my Life, my Way, my Light; in Thee
I live, I move, and by Thy beams I see.

Thou art my life: if Thou but turn away,
My life's a thousand deaths: Thou art my Way;
Without Thee, Lord, I travel not, but stray.

My Light Thou art; without Thy glorious sight,
Mine eyes are darkened with perpetual night.
My God, Thou art my Way, my Life, my Light.

Thou art my Way; I wander, if Thou fly:
Thou art my Light; if hid, how blind am I!
Thou art my Life; if thou withdraw, I die.

Mine eyes are blind and dark, I cannot see;
To whom, or whither, should my darkness flee,
But to the Light? And who's that Light but Thee?

My path is lost; my wandering steps do stray;
I cannot safely go, nor safely stay;
Whom should I seek but Thee, my Path, my Way?

* * * * *

Thou art the pilgrim's Path; the blind man's Eye;
The dead man's Life; on Thee my hopes rely;
If Thou remove, I err, I grope, I die.

Disclose Thy sun-beams; close Thy wings, and stay:
See, see how I am blind, and dead, and stray,
O Thou, that art my Light, my Life, my Way.

Francis Quarles, 1592-1644

EASTER

Rise, heart; thy Lord is risen. Sing His praise
      Without delayes,
Who takes thee by the hand, that thou likewise
      With Him mayst rise:
That, as His death calcinèd thee to dust,
His life may make thee gold, and much more, just.

Awake, my lute, and struggle for thy part
      With all thy art.
The crosse taught all wood to resound His name
      Who bore the same.
His stretchèd sinews taught all strings, what key
Is best to celebrate this most high day.

Consort both heart and lute, and twist a song
      Pleasant and long:
Or since all musick is but three parts vied
      And multiplied;
O let Thy blessed Spirit bear a part,
And make up our defects with His sweet art.

George Herbert, 1593-1633

MAN AND SAVIOUR: A DIALOGUE

Sweetest Saviour, if my soul
  Were but worth the having,
Quickly should I then controll
  Any thought of waving.
But when all my care and pains
Cannot give the name of gains
To thy wretch so full of stains,
What delight or hope remains?

'What, Child, is the ballance thine,
  Thine the poise and measure?
If I say, Thou shalt be mine;
  Finger not my treasure.
What the gains in having thee
Do amount to, onely he,
Who for man was sold, can see;
That transferr'd th' accounts to Me.'

But as I can see no merit,
  Leading to this favour:
So the way to fit me for it
  Is beyond my savour.
As the reason then is thine:
So the way is none of mine:
I disclaim the whole designe:
Sinne disclaims and I resigne.

'That is all, if that I could
  Get without repining;
And my clay, my creature, would
  Follow my resigning:
That as I did freely part
With my glorie and desert

Left all joyes to feel all smart—'
Ah! no more: thou break'st my heart.

George Herbert

Waving: ? in legal sense of declining the offer; savour: perception, under-
standing; desert: pronounced, and often spelt, desart. That is all, etc.:
That settles it, if only you submit without reservation, and copy My com-
plete renunciation.

PSALM FOR CHRISTMAS DAY

Behold the great Creator makes
    Himself an house of clay,
A robe of Virgin-flesh He takes
    Which He will wear for aye.

Hark, hark, the wise eternal Word
    Like a weak infant cries;
In form of servant is the Lord,
    And God in cradle lies.

This wonder struck the world amazed,
    It shook the starry frame;
Squadrons of spirits stood and gazed,
    Then down in troops they came.

Glad shepherds ran to view this sight;
    A quire of angels sings;
And eastern sages with delight
    Adore this King of kings.

Join then, all hearts that are not stone,
    And all our voices prove,
To celebrate this Holy One,
    The God of peace and love.

T. Pestel, 1595-1659

IF THE KING WERE COMING

Yet if His Majesty, our sovereign lord,
Should of his own accord
Friendly himself invite,
And say, 'I'll be your guest tomorrow night,'
How should we stir ourselves, call and command
All hands to work! 'Let no man idle stand!

'Set me fine Spanish tables in the hall,
See they be fitted all;
Let there be room to eat
And order taken that there want no meat.
See every sconce and candlestick made bright,
That without tapers they may give a light.

'Look to the presence: are the carpets spread,
The dazie o'er the head,
The cushions in the chairs,
And all the candles lighted on the stairs?
Perfume the chambers, and in any case
Let each man give attendance in his place.'

Thus, if the king were coming, would we do;
And 'twere good reason too;
For 'tis a duteous thing
To show all honour to an earthly king,
And after all our travail and our cost,
So he be pleased, to think no labour lost.

But at the coming of the King of Heaven
All's set at six and seven;
We wallow in our sin.
Christ cannot find a chamber in the inn.
We entertain Him always like a stranger,
And, as at first, still lodge Him in the manger.

Anonymous. Christ Church MS. ? early 17th century

[47]

THE LOVE OF CHRIST

Come, let's adore the King of Love,
    And King of Sufferings too;
For Love it was that brought Him down,
    And set Him here in woe.

Love drew Him from His Paradise,
    Where flowers that fade not grow;
And planted Him in our poor dust,
    Among us weeds below.

Here for a time this heavenly Plant
    Fairly grew up and thrived;
Diffused its sweetness all about,
    And all in sweetness lived.

But envious frosts and furious storms
    So long, so fiercely chide;
This tender Flower at last bowed down,
    And hung its head and died.

O narrow thoughts, and narrower speech,
    Here your defects confess;
The Life of Christ, the Death of God,
    How faintly you express!

Help, O thou Blessed Virgin Root,
    Whence this fair Flower did spring,
Help us to raise both heart and voice,
    And with more spirit sing.

John Austin, 1613-69

AT BETHLEHEM

Come, we shepherds, whose blest sight
  Hath met Love's noon in nature's night;
Come, lift we up our loftier song,
And wake the sun that lies too long.

Gloomy night embraced the place
  Where the noble Infant lay:
The Babe looked up and showed His face;
  In spite of darkness, it was day: —
It was Thy Day, Sweet! and did rise
Not from the east, but from Thine eyes.

We saw Thee in Thy balmy nest,
  Young dawn of our eternal day;
We saw Thine eyes break from their east,
  And chase the trembling shades away;
  We saw Thee, (and we bless the sight),
We saw Thee by Thine own sweet light.

Welcome, all wonders in one sight!
  Eternity shut in a span!
Summer in winter! Day in night!
Heaven in earth! and God in man!
Great Little One, whose all-embracing birth,
Lifts earth to heaven, stoops heaven to earth.

Richard Crashaw, 1613-50

ON THE CROSS

Thy restless feet now cannot go
   For us and our eternal good,
As they were ever wont. What though
   They swim, alas! in their own flood!

Thy hands to give Thou canst not lift,
   Yet will Thy hand still giving be;
It gives, but O, itself's the gift!
   It gives though bound, though bound 'tis free!

Richard Crashaw

HYMN FOR ADVENT

Lord, come away!
Why dost Thou stay?
Thy road is ready; and Thy paths made straight
With longing expectations wait
The consecration of Thy beauteous feet.
Ride on triumphantly; behold, we lay
Our lusts and proud wills in Thy way!

Hosanna! Welcome to our hearts! Lord, here
Thou hast a temple too; and full as dear
As that of Sion, and as full of sin:
Nothing but thieves and robbers dwell therein:
Enter, and chase them forth, and cleanse the floor:
Crucify them, that they may never more
Profane That holy place
Where Thou hast chose to set Thy face!
And then if our stiff tongues shall be
Mute in the praises of Thy Deity,
The stones out of the Temple wall
Shall cry aloud and call
Hosanna! And Thy glorious footsteps greet!

Jeremy Taylor, 1613-67

THE GOOD SHEPHERD

Christ who knows all His sheep
Will all in safety keep;
He will not lose His blood,
  Nor intercession:
Nor we the purchased good
  Of His dear Passion.

I know my God is just,
To Him I wholly trust
All that I have and am,
  All that I hope for.
All's sure and seen to Him,
  Which I here grope for.

Lord Jesus, take my spirit:
I trust Thy love and merit:
Take home this wandering sheep,
  For Thou hast sought it:
This soul in safety keep,
  For Thou hast bought it.

Richard Baxter, 1615-91

MORNING HYMN

What's this morn's bright eye to me,
If I see not Thine and Thee,
Fairer Jesu; in whose face
All my heaven is spread!—Alas,
Still I grovel in dead night,
Whilst I want Thy living light;
Dreaming with wide open eyes
Fond fantastic vanities.

Shine, my only Day-Star, shine;
So mine eyes shall wake by Thine;
So the dreams I grope in now
To clear visions all shall grow;
So my day shall measured be
By Thy grace's clarity;
So shall I discern the path
Thy sweet Law prescribèd hath;
For Thy ways cannot be shown
By any light but by Thine own.

Joseph Beaumont, 1616-99

PEACE

My soul, there is a country
    Afar beyond the stars,
Where stands a wingèd sentry
    All skilful in the wars.
There, above noise and danger,
    Sweet peace sits crowned with smiles,
And One born in a manger
    Commands the beauteous files.
He is thy gracious friend
    And (O my soul, awake!)
Did in pure love descend,
    To die here for thy sake.
If thou canst get but thither,
    There grows the flower of peace,
The rose that cannot wither,
    Thy fortress, and thy ease.
Leave then thy foolish ranges;
    For none can thee secure,
But One, who never changes,
    Thy God, thy Life, thy Cure.

Henry Vaughan, 1622-95

THE NATIVITY

Thou cam'st from heaven to earth, that we
Might go from earth to heaven with Thee:
And though Thou found'st no welcome here,
Thou didst provide us mansions there.
A stable was Thy court, and when
Men turned to beasts, beasts would be men:
They were Thy courtiers; others none;
And their poor manger was Thy throne.
No swaddling silks Thy limbs did fold,
Though Thou could'st turn Thy rags to gold.
No rockers waited on Thy birth,
No cradles stirred, no songs of mirth;
But her chaste lap and sacred breast,
Which lodged Thee first, did give Thee rest.

Henry Vaughan

THE THRONE

When with these eyes, closed now by Thee,
  But then restored,
The great and white throne I shall see
  Of my dread Lord;
And lowly kneeling—for the most
  Stiff, then must kneel—
Shall look on Him at whose high cost
  —Unseen—such joys I feel:—
Whatever arguments or skill
  Wise heads shall use,
Tears only and my blushes still
  I will produce.
And should those speechless beggars fail,
  Which oft have won,
Then taught by Thee I will prevail,
  And say, Thy will be done.

Henry Vaughan

THE RISEN CHRIST

Lord Jesus, with what sweetness and delights,
Sure, holy hopes, high joys, and quick'ning flights,
Dost Thou feed Thine! O Thou! the Hand that lifts
To Him, Who gives all good and perfect gifts,
Thy glorious, bright Ascension—though remov'd
So many ages from me—is so prov'd
And by Thy Spirit seal'd to me, that I
Feel me a sharer in Thy victory.

      I soar and rise
      Up to the skies,
        Leaving the world their day,
      And in my flight
      For the true light
        Go seeking all the way.

I greet Thy sepulchre, salute Thy grave,
That blest enclosure, where the angels gave
The first glad tidings of Thy early light,
And resurrection from the earth and night.
I see that morning in Thy convert's tears,
Fresh as the dew, which but this dawning wears.
I smell her spices; and her ointment yields
As rich a scent as the now primros'd fields:
The Day-star smiles, and light, with Thee deceas'd,
Now shines in all the chambers of the East.

    *   *   *   *   *

With these fair thoughts I move in this fair place,
And the last steps of my mild Master trace;
I see Him leading out His chosen train
All sad with tears; which like warm summer rain
In silent drops steal from their holy eyes,
Fix'd lately on the Cross, now on the skies.
And now, eternal Jesus, Thou dost heave
Thy blessed Hands to bless these Thou dost leave;
The Cloud doth now receive Thee, and their sight

Having lost Thee, behold two men in white!
Two and no more: 'What two attest, is true,'
Was Thine own answer to the stubborn Jew.
Come then, Thou faithful Witness! come, dear Lord,
Upon the clouds again to judge this world!

Henry Vaughan

AT HOME

Long did I toil and knew no earthly rest,
Far did I rove and found no certain home;
At last I sought them in His sheltering breast,
Who opes His arms and bids the weary come:
With Him I found a home, a rest divine,
And I since then am His, and He is mine.

The good I have is from His stores supplied,
The ill is only what He deems the best;
He for my friend I'm rich with nought beside,
And poor without Him, though of all possessed;
Changes may come, I take or I resign,
Content, while I am His, while He is mine.

Whate'er may change, in Him no change is seen,
A glorious Sun that wanes not nor declines,
Above the storms and clouds He walks serene,
And on His people's inward darkness shines;
All may depart, I fret not, nor repine,
While I my Saviour's am, while He is mine.

While here, alas! I know but half His love,
But half discern Him and but half adore;
But when I meet Him in the realms above
I hope to love Him better, praise Him more,
And feel, and tell, amid the choir divine,
How fully I am His and He is mine.

J. Quarles, 1624-65 and H. F. Lyte, 1793-1847

NO STORY SO DIVINE

My song is love unknown;
My Saviour's love to me;
Love to the loveless shown,
That they might lovely be.
    O who am I
       That for my sake,
       My Lord should take
    Frail flesh, and die?

He came from His blest Throne,
Salvation to bestow:
But men made strange, and none
The longed-for Christ would know.
    But O my Friend!
       My Friend indeed,
       Who at my need
    His life did spend.

Sometimes they strew His way,
And His sweet praises sing;
Resounding all the day,
Hosannas to their King.
    Then: Crucify!
       Is all their breath,
       And for His death
    They thirst and cry.

Why, what hath my Lord done?
What makes this rage and spite?
He made the lame to run,
He gave the blind their sight.
    Sweet injuries!
       Yet they at these
       Themselves displease,
    And 'gainst Him rise.

They rise and needs will have
My dear Lord made away;
A murderer they save;
The Prince of life they slay.
    Yet cheerful He
      To suffering goes,
      That He His foes
    From thence might free.

In life, no house, no home
My Lord on earth might have;
In death, no friendly tomb
But what a stranger gave.
    What may I say?
      Heav'n was His home;
      But mine the tomb
    Wherein He lay.

Here might I stay and sing,
No story so divine;
Never was love, dear King,
Never was grief like Thine.
    This is my Friend,
      In whose sweet praise
      I all my days
    Could gladly spend.

Samuel Crossman, c. 1624-83

CHRISTIAN LOSES HIS BURDEN

So I saw in my dream that just as Christian came up with the cross, his burden loosed from off his shoulders and fell from off his back, and began to tumble and so continued to do till it came to the mouth of the sepulchre, where it fell in, and I saw it no more. . . . Then Christian gave three leaps for joy and went on singing:

Thus far I did come laden with my sin;
Nor could aught ease the grief that I was in,
Till I came hither. What a place is this!
Must here be the beginning of my bliss?
Must here the burden fall from off my back?
Must here the strings that bound it to me crack?
Blessed cross! Blessed sepulchre! Blessed rather be
The Man that there was put to shame for me!

John Bunyan, 1628-88. FROM THE PILGRIM'S PROGRESS

PARABLES OF CHRIST

Go, worship at Immanuel's feet;
See, in His face what wonders meet;
Earth is too narrow to express
His worth, His glory, or His grace!

The whole creation can afford
But some faint shadows of my Lord;
Nature, to make His beauties known,
Must mingle colours not her own.

Is He compared to wine or bread?
Dear Lord, our souls would thus be fed;
That flesh, that dying blood of Thine,
Is Bread of Life, is heavenly Wine.

Is He a tree? The world receives
Salvation from His healing leaves;
That righteous Branch, that fruitful bough
Is David's root and offspring too.

Is He a rose? Not Sharon yields
Such fragrancy in all her fields;
Or if the lily He assume,
The valleys bless the rich perfume.

Is He a vine? His heavenly root
Supplies the boughs with life and fruit:
O let a lasting union join
My soul the branch to Christ the Vine.

Is He the head? Each member lives
And owns the vital power He gives;
The saints below and saints above
Joined by His Spirit and His love.

Is He a fountain? There I bathe,
And heal the plague of sin and death;
These waters all my soul renew,
And cleanse my spotted garments too.

Is He a fire? He'll purge my dross;
But the true gold sustains no loss:
Like a refiner shall He sit
And tread the refuse with His feet.

Is He a rock? How firm He proves!
The Rock of Ages never moves:
Yet the sweet streams that from Him flow
Attend us all the desert through.

Is He a Way? He leads to God;
The path is drawn in lines of blood;
There would I walk with hope and zeal
Till I arrive at Zion's hill.

Is He a door? I'll enter in;
Behold the pastures large and green!
A paradise divinely fair;
None but the sheep have freedom there.

Is He designed a corner-stone,
For men to build their heaven upon?
I'll make Him my foundation too,
Nor fear the plots of hell below.

Is He a temple? I adore
The indwelling majesty and power;
And still to His most holy place,
Whene'er I pray, I turn my face.

Is He a star? He breaks the night,
Piercing the shade with dawning light;
I know His glories from afar,
I know the bright, the morning Star!

Is He a sun? His beams are grace,
His course is joy and righteousness:
Nations rejoice when He appears
To chase their clouds and dry their tears.

Oh! let me climb those higher skies
Where storms and darkness never rise!
There He displays His powers abroad,
And shines and reigns, th' incarnate God.

Nor earth, nor seas, nor sun, nor stars,
Nor heaven His full resemblance bears:
His beauties we can never trace
Till we behold Him face to face.

Isaac Watts, 1674-1748

AT THE SEPULCHRE

Ye humble souls that seek the Lord,
　　Chase all your fears away;
And bow with pleasure down to see
　　The place where Jesus lay.

Thus low the Lord of life was brought;
　　Such wonders Love can do;
Thus cold in death that bosom lay,
　　Which throbb'd and bled for you.

Then raise your eyes, and tune your songs;
　　The Saviour lives again!
Not all the bolts and bars of death
　　The Conqueror could detain:

High o'er the angelic bands He rears
　　His once dishonoured head;
And through unnumber'd years He reigns,
　　Who dwelt among the dead.

Philip Doddridge, 1702-51

THE ENCOUNTER

In evil long I took delight,
  Unawed by shame or fear,
Till a new object struck my sight,
And stopped my wild career:
I saw One hanging on a tree
  In agonies and blood,
Who fixed His languid eyes on me,
  As near His cross I stood.

Sure never till my latest breath
  Can I forget that look:
It seemed to charge me with His death,
Though not a word He spoke:
My conscience felt and owned the guilt,
  And plunged me in despair;
I saw my sins His Blood had spilt
  And helped to nail Him there.

Alas! I knew not what I did!
  But now my tears are vain:
Where shall my trembling soul be hid?
  For I the Lord have slain!
A second look He gave, which said,
  'I freely all forgive;
This Blood is for thy ransom paid;
  I die, that thou mayst live.'

Thus, while His death my sin displays
  In all its blackest hue,
Such is the mystery of grace,
  It seals my pardon too.
With pleasing grief, and mournful joy,
  My spirit now is filled,
That I should such a life destroy,
  Yet live by Him I killed!

John Newton, 1725-1807

[67]

CHRIST THE HEALER

I was a stricken deer, that left the herd
Long since. With many an arrow deep infixt
My panting side was charged, when I withdrew
To seek a tranquil death in distant shades.
There was I found by One who had Himself
Been hurt by th' archers. In His side He bore,
And in His hands and feet, the cruel scars.
With gentle force soliciting the darts,
He drew them forth and healed, and bade me live.

William Cowper, 1731-1800. From THE TASK

WITHOUT HIM WAS NOT ANYTHING MADE

One spirit—His
Who wore the platted thorns with bleeding brows—
Rules universal nature. Not a flow'r
But shows some touch, in freckle, streak, or stain,
Of His unrivalled pencil. He inspires
Their balmy odours, and imparts their hues,
And bathes their eyes with nectar, and includes,
In grains as countless as the seaside sands,
The forms with which He sprinkles all the earth.
Happy who walks with Him! whom what he finds
Of flavour or of scent in fruit or flower,
Or what he views of beautiful or grand
In nature, from the broad majestic oak
To the green blade that twinkles in the sun,
Prompts with remembrance of a present God!

William Cowper

THE PRESENTATION IN THE TEMPLE

Simeon the just and the devout,
   Who frequent in the fane
Had for the Saviour waited long,
   But waited still in vain,

Came Heaven-directed at the hour
   When Mary held her Son;
He stretched forth his aged arms,
   While tears of gladness run:

With holy joy upon his face
   The good old father smiled,
While fondly in his withered arms
   He clasped the promised Child.

'At last my arms embrace my Lord;
   Now let their vigour cease;
At last my eyes my Saviour see,
   Now let them close in peace;

'The Star and Glory of the land
   Hath now begun to shine;
The morning that shall gild the globe
   Breaks on these eyes of mine!'

Michael Bruce, 1746-67

ON ANOTHER'S SORROW

Can I see another's woe
And not be in sorrow too?
Can I see another's grief
And not seek for kind relief?

Can I see a falling tear
And not feel my sorrow's share?
Can a father see his child
Weep, nor be with sorrow filled?

Can a mother sit and hear
An infant groan an infant fear?
No, no, never can it be,
Never, never can it be.

And can He who smiles on all
Hear the wren with sorrows small,
Hear the small bird's grief and care,
Hear the woes that infants bear,

And not sit beside the nest
Pouring pity in their breast,
And not sit the cradle near
Weeping tear on infant's tear,

And not sit both night and day
Wiping all our tears away?
O no! never can it be,
Never, never can it be.

He doth give His joy to all,
He becomes an infant small,
He becomes a man of woe,
He doth feel the sorrow too.

Think not thou canst sigh a sigh
And thy Maker is not by;
Think not thou canst weep a tear
And thy Maker is not near.

O! He gives to us His joy
That our grief He may destroy;
Till our grief is fled and gone
He doth sit by us and moan.

William Blake, 1757-1827

HIS FIRM ENDURANCE

I know with full assurance
  In whom I place my trust:
What proves its firm endurance
  When this world turns to dust.
I know what bides eternal
  Where all else shakes and falls,
When fraud from foes infernal
  Earth's shrewdest wits enthrals.

I know what never faileth
  But evermore endures;
A fort when hell assaileth
  In safety me secures:
The words of Christ my Saviour
  My refuge are and tower,
They show His grace and favour
  And shield in danger's hour.

My Rock and my Defender
  Right well my soul doth know:
All Heaven glows with His splendour,
  He rules His Church below.
Him seraphs with love burning
  Adore on bended knee:
His saints on earth are yearning
  For His epiphany.

And so with full assurance
  In Him I place my trust:
I'll prove His firm endurance
  When this world turns to dust.
When death's dark shades are o'er me
  He'll keep me in His hand
Till crowned with those in glory
  Beside His throne I stand.

Ernst Moritz Arndt, 1769-1860
  Tr. R. Birch Hoyle, 1875-1939

[73]

THOU ART TRUE

Not seldom, clad in radiant vest,
Deceitfully goes forth the Morn;
Not seldom Evening in the west
Sinks smilingly forsworn.

The smoothest seas will sometimes prove,
To the confiding Bark, untrue;
And if she trust the stars above,
They can be treacherous too.

But Thou art true, incarnate Lord,
Who didst vouchsafe for man to die;
Thy smile is sure, Thy plighted word
No change can falsify!

I bent before Thy gracious throne,
And ask'd for peace on suppliant knee;
And peace was given,—nor peace alone,
But Faith sublimed to ecstasy!

William Wordsworth, 1770-1850

When our heads are bowed with woe,
When our bitter tears o'erflow;
When we mourn the lost, the dear,
Gracious Son of Mary, hear!

Thou our throbbing flesh hast worn,
Thou our mortal griefs hast borne,
Thou hast shed the human tear:
Gracious Son of Mary, hear!

When the sullen death-bell tolls
For our own departed souls;
When our final doom is near,
Gracious Son of Mary, hear!

Thou hast bow'd the dying head;
Thou the blood of life hast shed;
Thou hast fill'd a mortal bier:
Gracious Son of Mary hear!

When the heart is sad within
With the thought of all its sin;
When the spirit shrinks with fear,
Gracious Son of Mary, hear!

Thou the shame, the grief hast known,
Though the sins were not Thine own;
Thou hast deign'd their load to bear—
Gracious Son of Mary, hear!

Henry Hart Milman, 1791-1868

CALVARY

They gave Him to drink wine mingled with myrrh: but He received it not. Mark 15.23.

'Fill high the bowl, and spice it well, and pour
The dews oblivious: for the Cross is sharp,
   The Cross is sharp, and He
   Is tenderer than a lamb.

'He wept by Lazarus' grave—how will He bear
This bed of anguish? and His pale weak form
   Is worn with many a watch
   Of sorrow and unrest.

'His sweat last night was as great drops of blood,
And the sad burthen pressed Him so to earth,
   The very torturers paused
   To help Him on His way.

'Fill high the bowl, benumb His aching sense
With medicined sleep.'—O awful in Thy woe!
   The parching thirst of death
   Is on Thee, and Thou triest

The slumbrous potion bland, and wilt not drink:
Not sullen, nor in scorn, like haughty man
   With suicidal hand
   Putting his solace by:

But as at first Thine all-pervading look
Saw from Thy Father's bosom to th' abyss,
   Measuring in calm presage
   The infinite descent;

So to the end, though now of mortal pangs
Made heir, and emptied of Thy glory awhile,
   With unaverted eye
   Thou meetest all the storm.

Thou wilt feel all, that Thou mayst pity all;
And rather wouldst Thou wrestle with strong pain,
    Than overcloud Thy soul,
    So clear in agony,

Or lose one glimpse of Heaven before the time.
O most entire and perfect sacrifice,
    Renewed in every pulse
    That on the tedious Cross

Told the long hours of death, as, one by one,
The life-strings of that tender heart gave way;
    E'en sinners, taught by Thee,
    Look Sorrow in the face,

And bid her freely welcome, unbeguiled
By false kind solaces, and spells of earth:—
    And yet not all unsoothed:
    For when was Joy so dear,

As the deep calm that breathed, 'Father, forgive',
Or, 'Be with Me in paradise today'?
    And, though the strife be sore,
    Yet in His parting breath

Love masters agony; the soul that seemed
Forsaken, feels her present God again,
    And in her Father's arms
    Contented dies away.

John Keble, 1792-1866

BLESSED ARE THEY THAT HAVE NOT SEEN

We were not by when Jesus came;
    But round us, far and near,
We see His trophies, and His name
    In choral echoes hear.
In a fair ground our lot is cast,
As in the solemn week that past,
While some might doubt, but all adored,
Ere the whole widow'd Church had seen her risen Lord.

Then, gliding through th' opening door,
    Smooth without step or sound,
'Peace to your souls,' He said—no more—
    They own Him, kneeling round.
Eye, ear, and hand, and loving heart,
Body and soul in every part,
Successive made His witnesses that hour,
Cease not in all the world to shew His saving power.

Is there, on earth, a spirit frail,
    Who fears to take their word,
Scarce daring, through the twilight pale,
    To think he sees the Lord?
With eyes too tremblingly awake
To bear with dimness for His sake?
Read and confess the Hand Divine
That drew thy likeness here so true in every line.

For all thy rankling doubts so sore,
    Love thou the Saviour still,
Him for thy Lord and God adore,
    And ever do His will.
Though vexing thoughts may seem to last,
Let not thy soul be quite o'ercast;—
Soon will He shew thee all His wounds, and say,
'Long have I known thy name—know thou My face alway.'

John Keble

[78]

THE STRANGER

Ay, once a Stranger blest the earth
  Who never caused a heart to mourn,
Whose very voice gave sorrow mirth—
  And how did earth His worth return?
It spurned Him from its lowliest lot,
The meanest station owned Him not;

An outcast thrown in sorrow's way,
  A fugitive that knew no sin,
Yet in lone places forced to stray—
  Men would not take the Stranger in.
Yet peace, though much Himself He mourned,
Was all to others He returned.

    *   *   *   *

His presence was a peace to all,
  He bade the sorrowful rejoice.
Pain turned to pleasure at His call,
  Health lived and issued from His voice.
He healed the sick and sent abroad
The dumb rejoicing in the Lord.

The blind met daylight in His eye,
  The joys of everlasting day;
The sick found health in His reply;
  The cripple threw his crutch away.
Yet He with troubles did remain
And suffered poverty and pain.

Yet none could say of wrong He did,
  And scorn was ever standing by;
Accusers by their conscience chid,
  When proof was sought, made no reply.
Yet without sin He suffered more
Than ever sinners did before.

And yet for sin He suffered all,
    To set the world-imprisoned free,
To cheer the weary when they call—
    And who could such a Stranger be?
The God, the Saviour from on high
That aids the feeble. Need I sigh?

John Clare, 1793-1864

THE SIGHT OF CHRIST

As Gerontius dies, his guardian angel conducts his soul
to the presence of Christ.

When then—if such thy lot—thou seest thy Judge,
The sight of Him will kindle in thy heart
All tender, gracious reverential thoughts.
Thou wilt be sick with love, and yearn for Him,
And feel as though thou couldst but pity Him,
That one so sweet should e'er have placed Himself
At disadvantage such, as to be used
So vilely by a being so vile as thee.
There is a pleading in His pensive eyes
Will pierce thee to the quick, and trouble thee.
And thou wilt hate and loathe thyself; for, though
Now sinless, thou wilt feel that thou hast sinned,
As never thou didst feel; and wilt desire
To slink away, and hide thee from His sight;
And yet wilt have a longing aye to dwell
Within the beauty of His countenance.
And these two pains, so counter and so keen,—
The longing for Him, when thou seest Him not;
The shame of self at thought of seeing Him,—
Will be thy veriest, sharpest purgatory.

John Henry Newman, 1801-90,
from THE DREAM OF GERONTIUS

STRONG SON OF GOD

Strong Son of God, immortal Love,
　　Whom we, that have not seen Thy face,
　　By faith, and faith alone, embrace,
Believing where we cannot prove;

Thine are these orbs of light and shade;
　　Thou madest life in man and brute;
　　Thou madest Death; and lo, Thy foot,
Is on the skull that Thou hast made.

Thou wilt not leave us in the dust;
　　Thou madest man, he knows not why;
　　He thinks he was not made to die;
And Thou hast made him: Thou art just.

Thou seemest human and divine,
　　The highest, holiest manhood, Thou;
　　Our wills are ours, we know not how;
Our wills are ours, to make them Thine.

Our little systems have their day;
　　They have their day, and cease to be:
　　They are but broken lights of Thee,
And Thou, O Lord, art more than they.

We have but faith; we cannot know;
　　For knowledge is of things we see;
　　And yet we trust it comes from Thee,
A beam in darkness: let it grow.

Let knowledge grow from more to more,
　　But more of reverence in us dwell;
　　That mind and soul, according well,
May make one music as before,

But vaster. We are fools and slight;
   We mock Thee when we do not fear:
   But help Thy foolish ones to bear;
Help Thy vain worlds to bear Thy light.

Alfred Tennyson, 1809-92, from IN MEMORIAM

THE WORD HAD BREATH

For wisdom dealt with mortal powers,
   Where truth in closest words shall fail,
   Where truth embodied in a tale
Shall enter in at lowly doors.

And so the Word had breath, and wrought
   With human hands the creed of creeds
   In loveliness of perfect deeds
More strong than all poetic thought,

Which he may read that binds the sheaf,
   Or builds the house, or digs the grave,
   And those wild eyes that watch the wave
In roarings round the coral reef.

Alfred Tennyson, from IN MEMORIAM

SAUL AND DAVID

David's eagerness to help the mad king in his distress, at any cost to himself, leads him to foreshadow God's purpose of redemption in Christ.

'Do I find love so full in my nature, God's ultimate gift,
That I doubt His own love can compete with it? here, the parts shift?
Here, the creature surpass the Creator, the end, what began?—
Would I fain in my impotent yearning do all for this man,
And dare doubt He alone shall not help him, who yet alone can?
Would it ever have entered my mind, the bare will, much less power,
To bestow on this Saul what I sang of, the marvellous dower
Of the life he was gifted and filled with? to make such a soul,
Such a body, and then such an earth for insphering the whole?
And doth it not enter my mind (as my warm tears attest)
These good things being given, to go on, and give one more, the best?
Ay, to save and redeem and restore him, maintain at the height
This perfection,—succeed, with life's dayspring, death's minute of night?
Interpose at the difficult minute, snatch Saul, the mistake,
Saul, the failure, the ruin he seems now,—and bid him awake
From the dream, the probation, the prelude, to find himself set
Clear and safe in new light and new life,—a new harmony yet
To be run, and continued, and ended—who knows?—or endure!
The man taught enough, by life's dream, of the rest to make sure.

By the pain-throb, triumphantly winning intensified bliss,
And the next world's reward and repose, by the struggle in
    this.

'I believe it! 'tis Thou, God, that givest, 'tis I who receive:
In the first is the last, in Thy will is my power to believe.
All's one gift: Thou canst grant it moreover, as prompt to
    my prayer,
As I breathe out this breath, as I open these arms to the air.
From Thy will, stream the worlds, life and nature, Thy
    dread Sabaoth:
I will?—the mere atoms despise me! Why am I not loth
To look that, even that in the face too? why is it I dare
Think but lightly of such impuissance? what stops my
    despair?
This:—'tis not what man does which exalts him, but what
    man would do!
See the king—I would help him but cannot, the wishes fall
    through.
Could I wrestle to save him from sorrow, grow poor to
    enrich,
To fill up his life, starve my own out, I would—knowing
    which,
I know that my service is perfect.—Oh speak through me
    now!
Would I suffer for him that I love? So wilt Thou—so wilt
    Thou!
So shall crown Thee the topmost, ineffablest, uttermost
    crown—
And Thy love fill infinitude wholly, nor leave up nor down
One spot for the creature to stand in! It is by no breath,
Turn of eye, wave of hand, that salvation joins issue with
    death!
As Thy love is discovered almighty, almighty be proved
Thy power that exists with and for it, of being beloved!
He who did most, shall bear most; the strongest shall stand
    the most weak.

'Tis the weakness in strength that I cry for! my flesh that I
    seek
In the Godhead! I seek and I find it. O Saul, it shall be
A Face like my face that receives thee: a Man like to me
Thou shalt love and be loved by, for ever! A hand like this
    hand
Shall throw open the gates of new life to thee. 'See the
    Christ stand!'

Robert Browning, 1812-89

THE ALL-GREAT IS THE ALL-LOVING

So, the All-great were the All-loving too—
So, through the thunder comes a human voice
Saying, 'O heart I made, a heart beats here!
Face My hands fashioned, see it in Myself.
Thou hast no power, nor may'st conceive of Mine,
But love I gave thee, with Myself to love,
And thou must love Me who have died for thee.'

Robert Browning

I

Ashes to ashes, dust to dust;
As of the unjust, also of the just—
Yea, of that Just One too.
This is the one sad Gospel that is true,
Christ is not risen.

Is He not risen, and shall we not rise?
Oh, we unwise!
What did we dream, what wake we to discover?
Ye hills, fall on us, and ye mountains, cover!
In darkness and great gloom
Come ere we thought it is *our* day of doom,
From the cursed world which is one tomb,
Christ is not risen!

Eat, drink, and die, for we are men deceived.
Of all the creatures under heaven's wide cope
We are most hopeless who had once most hope.
We are most wretched that had most believed.
Christ is not risen.

Eat, drink, and play, and think that this is bliss!
There is no Heaven but this!
There is no Hell:—
Save Earth, which serves the purpose doubly well,
Seeing it visits still
With equallest apportionment of ill
Both good and bad alike, and brings to one same dust
The unjust and the just
With Christ who is not risen.

Weep not beside the Tomb,
Ye women, unto whom

He was great solace while ye tended Him;
   Ye who with napkin o'er His head
And folds of linen round each wounded limb
   Laid out the Sacred Dead.
And thou that bar'st Him in thy wondering Womb,
Yea, Daughters of Jerusalem, depart,
Bind up as best ye may your own sad bleeding heart;
Go to your homes, your living children tend,
       Your earthly spouses love;
       Set your affections *not* on things above,
Which moth and rust corrupt, which quickliest come to end:
Or pray, if pray ye must, and pray, if pray ye can,
For death; since dead is He whom ye deemed more than man,
       Who is not risen, no,
       But lies and moulders low,
       Who is not risen.

And oh, good men of ages yet to be
Who shall believe *because* ye did not see,
       Oh, be ye warned, be wise!
       No more with pleading eyes
       And sobs of strong desire
Unto the empty vacant void aspire,
Seeking another and impossible birth
That is not of your own and only Mother Earth.
But if there is no other life for you,
Sit down and be content, since this must even do;
       He is not risen.

       Here on our Easter Day
We rise, we come, and lo! we find Him not;
Gardener nor other on the sacred spot,
Where they have laid Him there is none to say!
No sound, nor in, nor out; no word
Of where to seek the dead or meet the living Lord;
There is no glistering of an angel's wings
There is no voice of heavenly clear behest;

Let us go hence, and think upon these things
In silence, which is best.
       Is He not risen? No—
       But lies and moulders low—
       Christ is not risen.

II

. . . . . .
So in the sinful street, abstracted and alone
I with my secret self held communing of my own.
So in the southern city spake the tongue
  Of one that somewhat overwildly sung;
  But in a later hour I sat and heard
Another voice that spake, another graver word.
Weep not, it bade, whatever hath been said,
Though He be dead, He is not dead.
       In the true Creed
       He is yet risen indeed,
       Christ is yet risen.

Sit if ye will, sit down upon the ground,
Yet not to weep and wail, but calmly look around.
       Whate'er befell,
       Earth is not hell;
  Now, too, as when it first began,
  Life is yet Life and Man is Man.
For all that breathe beneath the heaven's high cope,
Joy with grief mixes, with despondence hope.
Hope conquers cowardice, joy, grief,
Or at the least, faith unbelief.
       Though dead, not dead,
       Not gone, though fled;
       Not lost, not vanished.

In the great Gospel and true Creed
He is yet risen indeed;
   Christ is yet risen.

Arthur Hugh Clough, 1819-61

O MY COMRADE

My spirit to yours, dear Brother,
Do not mind because many sounding Your name do not
    understand You,
I do not sound Your name, but I understand You.
I specify You with joy, O my Comrade, to salute You, and
    to salute those who are with You before and since,
    and those to come also,
That we may all labour together transmitting the same
    charge and succession,
We few equals indifferent of lands, indifferent of times,
We, enclosers of all continents, all castes, allowers of all
    theologies,
Compassionaters, perceivers, rapport of men,
We walk silent among disputes and assertions, but reject
    not the disputers nor anything that is asserted,
We hear the bawling and din, we are reached at by divisions,
    jealousies, recriminations on every side,
They close peremptorily upon us to surround us, my
    Comrade,
Yet we walk upheld, free, the whole world over, journeying
    up and down till we make our ineffaccable mark upon
    time and the diverse eras,
Till we saturate time and eras, that the men and women of
    races, ages to come, may prove brethren and lovers as
    we are.

Walt Whitman, 1819-92

THE GOOD SHEPHERD WITH THE KID

'He saves the sheep, the goats He doth not save!'
So rang Tertullian's sentence, on the side
Of that unpitying Phrygian sect which cried:
'Him can no fount of fresh forgiveness lave,

Who sins, once washed by the baptismal wave!'
So spake the fierce Tertullian. But she sighed,
The infant Church! of love she felt the tide
Stream on her from her Lord's yet recent grave.

And then she smiled; and in the Catacombs,
With eye suffused but heart inspirèd true,
On those walls subterranean, where she hid

Her head 'mid ignominy, death and tombs,
She her Good Shepherd's hasty image drew—
And on His shoulders, not a lamb, a kid.

Matthew Arnold, 1822-88

THE PRESENCE OF CHRIST

When thou turn'st away from ill,
Christ is this side of thy hill.

When thou turnest toward good,
Christ is walking in thy wood.

When thy heart says 'Father, pardon!'
Then the Lord is in thy garden.

When stern duty wakes to watch,
Then His hand is on the latch.

But when hope thy song doth rouse,
Then the Lord is in the house.

When to love is all thy wit,
Christ doth at thy table sit.

When God's will is thy heart's pole,
Then is Christ thy very soul.

George Macdonald, 1824-1905

THE SWEEPER OF THE FLOOR

Methought that in a solemn church I stood.
Its marble acres, worn with knees and feet,
Lay spread from door to door, from street to street.
Midway the form hung high upon the rood
Of Him who gave His life to be our good;
Beyond, priests flitted, bowed, and murmured meet,
Among the candles shining still and sweet.
Men came and went, and worshipped as they could—
And still their dust a woman with her broom,
Bowed to her work, kept sweeping to the door.
Then saw I, slow through all the pillared gloom,
Across the church a silent figure come:
'Daughter,' it said, 'thou sweepest well My floor!'
'It is the Lord!' I cried, and saw no more.

George Macdonald

THE GOOD SHEPHERD

O Shepherd with the bleeding feet,
  Good Shepherd with the pleading voice,
    What seekest Thou from hill to hill?
Sweet were the valley pastures, sweet
  The sound of flocks that bleat their joys,
    And eat and drink at will.
Is one worth seeking, when Thou hast of Thine
        Ninety and nine?—

How should I stay My bleeding feet,
  How should I hush My pleading voice?
    I who chose death and clomb a hill,
Accounting gall and wormwood sweet,
  That hundredfold might bud My joys
    For love's sake and good will.
I seek My one, for all there bide of Mine
        Ninety and nine.

Christina Rossetti, 1830-94

THE OXEN

Christmas Eve, and twelve of the clock.
  'Now they are all on their knees',
An elder said as we sat in a flock
  By the embers in hearthside ease.

We pictured the meek mild creatures where
  They dwelt in their strawy pen,
Nor did it occur to one of us there
  To doubt they were kneeling then.

So fair a fancy few would weave
  In these years! Yet, I feel,
If someone said on Christmas Eve,
  'Come; see the oxen kneel

'In the lonely barton by yonder coomb
  Our childhood used to know,'
I should go with him in the gloom,
  Hoping it might be so.

Thomas Hardy, 1840-1928

A frosty Christmas Eve
  when the stars were shining
Fared I forth alone
  where westward falls the hill,
And forth from many a village
  in the water'd valley
Distant music reach'd me,
  peals of bells aringing.
The constellated sounds
  ran sprinkling on earth's floor
As the dark vault above
  with stars was spangled o'er.

Then sped my thoughts to keep
  that first Christmas of all
When the shepherds watching
  by their folds ere the dawn
Heard music in the fields
  and marvelling could not tell
Whether it were angels
  or the bright stars singing.

Now blessed be the tow'rs
  that crown England so fair,
That stand up strong in prayer
  unto God for our souls:
Blessed be their founders
  (said I) an' our country folk
Who are ringing for Christ
  in the belfries tonight
With arms lifted to clutch
  the rattling ropes that race
Into the dark above
  and the mad romping din.

But to me heard afar
    it was starry music,
Angels' song comforting
    as the comfort of Christ
When he spake tenderly
    to his sorrowful flock:
The old words came to me
    by the riches of time
Mellow'd and transfigur'd
    as I stood on the hill
Heark'ning in the aspect
    of th' eternal silence.

Robert Bridges, 1844-1930

CHRIST AND THE PAGAN

I had no god but these,
The sacerdotal trees,
And they uplifted me.
'I hung upon a Tree.'

The sun and moon I saw,
And reverential awe
Subdued me day and night.
'I am the perfect Light.'

Within a lifeless stone—
All other gods unknown—
I sought divinity.
'The Corner-stone am I.'

For sacrificial feast,
I slaughtered man and beast,
Red recompense to gain.
'So I, a Lamb, was slain.'

'Yea; such my hungering grace
That whereso'er My face
Is hidden, none may grope
Beyond eternal hope.'

John Bannister Tabb, 1845-1909

NO SUDDEN THING

No sudden thing of glory and fear
Was the Lord's coming; but the dear
  Slow nature's days followed each other
   To form the Saviour from His mother—
One of the children of the year.

The earth, the rain, received the trust,—
The sun and dews, to frame the Just.
  He drew His daily life from these
   According to His own decrees,
Who makes man from the fertile dust.

Sweet summer and the winter wild,
These brought Him forth, the undefiled.
  The happy springs renewed again
   His daily bread, the growing grain,
The food and raiment of the child.

Alice Meynell, 1850-1922

HE ROSE AGAIN

All night had shouts of men and cry
   Of woeful women filled His way;
Until that noon of sombre sky
   On Friday, clamour and display
Smote Him; no solitude had He,
No silence, since Gethsemane.

Public was death; but power, but might,
   But life again, but victory,
Were hushed within the dead of night,
   The shuttered dark, the secrecy.
And all alone, alone, alone
He rose again behind the stone.

Alice Meynell

E TENEBRIS

Come down, O Christ, and help me! reach Thy hand,
For I am drowning in a stormier sea
Than Simon on the lake of Galilee:
The wine of life is spilt upon the sand,
My heart is as some famine-murdered land
Whence all good things have perished utterly,
And well I know my soul in Hell must lie
If I this night before God's throne should stand.
'He sleeps perchance, or rideth to the chase,
Like Baal, when his prophets howled that name
From morn to noon on Carmel's smitten height.'
Nay, peace, I shall behold, before the night,
The feet of brass, the robe more white than flame,
The wounded hands, the weary human face.

Oscar Wilde, 1856-1900

THE LAMB OF GOD

All in the April evening
  April airs were abroad,
The sheep with their little lambs
  Passed me by on the road.

The sheep with their little lambs
  Passed me by on the road;
All in the April evening
  I thought on the Lamb of God.

The lambs were weary, and crying
  With a weak and human cry.
I thought on the Lamb of God
  Going meekly to die.

Up in the blue, blue mountains
  Dewy pastures are sweet;
Rest for the little bodies,
  Rest for the little feet.

But for the Lamb of God
  Up on the hill-top green,
Only a cross of shame
  Two stark crosses between.

All in the April evening
  April airs were abroad,
I saw the sheep with their lambs
  And thought on the Lamb of God.

Katherine Tynan Hinkson, 1859-1931

THE HOUND OF HEAVEN

I fled Him, down the nights and down the days;
I fled Him, down the arches of the years;
I fled Him, down the labyrinthine ways
  Of my own mind; and in the mist of tears
I hid from Him, and under running laughter.
        Up vistaed hopes I sped;
        And shot, precipitated,
Adown Titanic glooms of chasmèd fears,
  From those strong Feet that followed, followed after.
        But with unhurrying chase
        And unperturbèd pace,
  Deliberate speed, majestic instancy,
        They beat—and a Voice beat
        More instant than the Feet—
'All things betray thee, who betrayest Me.'

*   *   *   *   *

        Now of that long pursuit
        Comes on at hand the bruit;
  That Voice is round me like a bursting sea:
        'And is thy earth so marred,
        Shattered in shard on shard?
  Lo, all things fly thee, for thou fliest Me!
  Strange, piteous, futile thing,
Wherefore should any set thee love apart
Seeing none but I makes much of nought' (He said),
'And human love needs human meriting:
  How hast thou merited—
Of all man's clotted clay the dingiest clot?
  Alack, thou knowest not
How little worthy of any love thou art!
Whom wilt thou find to love ignoble thee
  Save Me, save only Me?
All which I took from thee I did but take,
  Not for thy harms,

[106]

But just that thou might'st seek it in My arms.
  All which thy child's mistake
Fancies as lost, I have stored for thee at home:
  Rise, clasp My hand and come.'

    Halts by me that footfall:
    Is my gloom, after all,
  Shade of His hand, outstretched caressingly?
    'Ah, fondest, blindest, weakest,
    I am He whom thou seekest!
  Thou dravest love from thee, who dravest Me.'

Francis Thompson, 1859-1907

GOOD FRIDAY IN MY HEART

Good Friday in my heart! Fear and affright!
My thoughts are the disciples when they fled,
My words the words that priest and soldier said,
My deed the spear to desecrate the dead.
And day, Thy death therein, is changed to night.

Then Easter in my heart sends up the sun.
My thoughts are Mary, when she turned to see,
My words are Peter, answering, 'Lov'st thou me?'
My deeds are all Thine own drawn close to Thee,
And night and day, since Thou dost rise, are one.

Mary Elizabeth Coleridge, 1861-1907

A PRAYER FOR THE HEALING OF THE WOUNDS OF CHRIST

(For Advent)

Is not the work done? Nay, for still the Scars
Are open; still Earth's Pain stands deified,
    With Arms spread wide:
And still, like falling stars,
    Its Blood-drops strike the doorposts, where abide
    The watchers with the Bride,
To wait the final coming of their kin,
And hear the sound of kingdoms gathering in.

While Earth wears wounds, still must Christ's Wounds
        remain
Whom Love made Life, and of Whom Life made Pain,
    And of Whom Pain made Death.
    No breath,
Without Him, sorrow draws; no feet
    Wax weary, and no hands hard labour bear,
    But He doth wear
The travail and the heat:
Also, for all things perishing, He saith,
'*My* grief, *My* pain, *My* death.'

O kindred Constellation of bright stars,
    Ye shall not last for aye!
    Far off there dawns a comfortable day
Of healing for those Scars:
    When, faint in glory, shall be wiped away
        Each planetary fire,
Now, all the aching way the balm of Earth's desire!

For from the healèd nations there shall come
The healing touch: the blind, the lamed, the dumb,
    With sight, and speed, and speech,
    And ardent reach

Of yearning hands shall cover up from sight
Those Imprints of a night
For ever past. And all the Morians' lands
Shall stretch out hands of healing to His Hands.
    While to His Feet
    The timid, sweet
Four-footed ones of earth shall come and lay,
Forever by, the sadness of their day:
    And, they being healed, healing spring from them.
So for the Stem
And Rod of Jesse, roots and trees and flowers,
Touched with compassionate powers,
    Shall cause the thorny Crown
    To blossom down
        Laurel and bay.

        So lastly to His Side,
Stricken when, from the Body that had died,
Going down He saw sad souls being purified,
    Shall rise, out of the deeps no man
    Can sound or scan,
The morning star of Heaven that once fell
And fashioned Hell:—
    Now, star to star
    Mingling to melt where shadeless glories are.

O Earth, seek deep, and gather up thy soul,
And come from high and low, and near and far,
And make Christ whole!

Laurence Housman, 1865-1959

I WOULD SHOW THEE CHRIST

FRANCIS I would show thee Christ, Soldan. Or if by that name thou know Him not, then by His other name which is Love, wherein also dwell Joy and Peace. This I have come to show.

SOLDAN Yea: speak!

FRANCIS
Oh, hearken, for this is wonder!
Light looked down and beheld Darkness.
'Thither will I go,' said Light.
Peace looked down and beheld War.
'Thither will I go,' said Peace.
Love looked down and beheld Hatred.
'Thither will I go,' said Love.
So Light came and shone.
So came Peace and gave Rest.
So came Love and brought Life.
And the Word was made flesh and dwelt among us.

Laurence Housman. FROM LITTLE PLAYS OF ST FRANCIS

A GUEST WITHIN A GRAVE

Pilate and Caiaphas
They have brought this thing to pass—
That a Christ the Father gave,
Should be a guest within a grave.

Church and State have willed to last
This tyranny not over-past;
His dark southern brows around
They a wreath of briars have bound,
In His dark despised hands
Writ in sores their writing stands.

By strait starlit ways I creep,
Caring while the careless sleep,
Bearing balms, and flow'rs to crown
That poor head the stone holds down,
Through some crack or crevice dim
I would reach my sweets to him.

Easter suns they rise and set,
But that stone is steadfast yet:
Past my lifting 'tis, but I
When 'tis lifted would be nigh.
I believe, whate'er they say,
The sun shall dance on Easter Day,
And I that through thick twilight grope
With balms of faith, and flow'rs of hope,
Shall lift mine eyes and see that stone
Stir and shake, if not be gone.

Arthur Shearly Cripps, 1869-1952

OUR LADY

They crucified Him on Calvary
   Upon an April day;
And because He had been her little son
   She followed Him all the way.

Our Lady stood beside the Cross,
   A little space apart,
And when she heard our Lord cry out
   A sword went through her heart.

Hilaire Belloc, 1870-1953

JESUS OF THE SCARS

If we never sought, we seek Thee now;
  Thine eyes burn through the dark, our only stars;
We must have sight of thorn-pricks on Thy brow,
  We must have Thee, O Jesus of the scars.

The heavens frighten us; they are too calm;
  In all the universe we have no place.
Our wounds are hurting us; where is the balm?
  Lord Jesus, by Thy scars we claim Thy grace.

If when the doors are shut, Thou drawest near,
  Only reveal those hands, that side of Thine;
We know today what wounds are, have no fear,
  Show us Thy scars, we know the countersign.

The other gods were strong; but Thou wast weak;
  They rode, but Thou didst stumble to a throne;
But to our wounds God's wounds alone can speak,
  And not a god has wounds, but Thou alone.

Edward Shillito, 1872-1948

THE PRAYER OF A MODERN THOMAS

If Thou, O God, the Christ didst leave,
In Him, not Thee, I do believe;
  To Jesus dying all alone,
  To His dark Cross, not Thy bright Throne,
My hopeless hands will cleave.

But if it was Thy love that died,
Thy voice that in the darkness cried,
  The print of nails I long to see,
  In Thy hands, God, who fashioned me.
Show me *Thy* piercèd side.

Edward Shillito

HIS BLOOD UPON THE ROSE

I see His blood upon the rose
And in the stars the glory of His eyes,
His body gleams amid eternal snows,
His tears fall from the skies.

I see His face in every flower;
The thunder and the singing of the birds
Are but His voice—and carven by His power
Rocks are His written words.

All pathways by His feet are worn,
His strong heart stirs the ever-beating sea,
His crown of thorns is twined with every thorn,
His cross is every tree.

Joseph Mary Plunkett, 1887-1916

THE EVERLASTING MERCY

Saul Kane has been converted from a life of drunkenness and sensuality.
He is watching 'Old Callow at his autumn ploughing'.

O wet red swathe of earth laid bare,
O truth, O strength, O gleaming share,
O patient eyes that watch the goal,
O ploughman of the sinner's soul,
O Jesus, drive the coulter deep
To plough my living man from sleep.

*   *   *   *   *

I kneeled there in the muddy fallow,
I knew that Christ was there with Callow,
That Christ was standing there with me,
That Christ had taught me what to be,
That I should plough, and as I ploughed
My Saviour Christ would sing aloud,
And as I drove the clods apart
Christ would be ploughing in my heart,
Through rest-harrow and bitter roots,
Through all my bad life's rotten fruits.

O Christ who holds the open gate,
O Christ who drives the furrow straight,
O Christ, the plough, O Christ, the laughter
Of holy white birds flying after,
Lo, all my heart's field red and torn,
And Thou wilt bring the young green corn.
The young green corn divinely springing,
The young green corn for ever singing;
And when the field is fresh and fair
Thy blessèd feet shall glitter there.
And we will walk the weeded field,
And tell the golden harvest's yield,
The corn that makes the holy bread

By which the soul of man is fed,
The holy bread, the food unpriced,
Thy everlasting mercy, Christ.

Thy share will jar on many a stone,
Thou wilt not let me stand alone,
And I shall feel (Thou wilt not fail)
Thy hand on mine upon the hale.

John Masefield, 1875-

CONVERSION

NICODEMUS
    But tell me why; why did you follow Him?

JOHN
    I think it was our feet that followed Him;
    It was our feet; our hearts were too afraid.
    Perhaps indeed it was not in our choice;
    He tells us that we have not chosen Him,
    But He has chosen us. I only know
    That as we followed Him that day He called us
    We were not walking on the earth at all;
    It was another world,
    Where everything was new and strange and shining;
    We pitied men and women at their business,
    For they knew nothing of what we knew—

NICODEMUS
    Perhaps it was some miracle He did.

JOHN
    It was indeed; more miracles than one;
    I was not blind and yet He gave me sight;
    I was not deaf and yet He gave me hearing;
    Nor was I dead, yet me He raised to life.

Andrew Young, 1885-. From NICODEMUS

EPIPHANY

It was a king of Negro-land,
  A king of China-town,
And an old prince of Iran,
  Who to the Child kneeled down.

It was a king of blackamoors,
  A king of men slant-eyed,
A lord among sun-worshippers,
  Who at the New-born spied.

It was a king with savage eyes,
  King with a queer pig-tail,
King with a high and sunlit brow,
  Who bade the New-born 'Hail!'

Back rode they to one country,
  One spiritual land,
Three kings of my soul's country,
  Who touched the New-born's hand.

Charles Williams, 1886-1945

THE MOMENT OF MEANING

Then came, at a predetermined moment, a moment in time
    and of time,
A moment not out of time, but in time, in what we call
    history: transecting, bisecting the world of time, a
    moment in time but not like a moment of time,
A moment in time but time was made through that moment;
    for without the meaning there is no time, and that
    moment of time gave the meaning.
Then it seemed as if men must proceed from light to light,
    in the light of the Word,
Through the Passion and Sacrifice saved in spite of their
    negative being:
Bestial as ever before, carnal, self-seeking as always before,
    selfish and purblind as ever before,
Yet always struggling, always reaffirming, always resuming
    their march on the way that was lit by the light;
Often halting, loitering, straying, delaying, returning, yet
    following no other way.
But it seems that something has happened that has never
    happened before: though we know not just when, or
    why, or where.
Men have left God not for other gods, they say, but for no
    god; and this has never happened before
That men both deny gods and worship gods, professing first
    Reason,
And then Money, and Power, and what they call Life, or
    Race, or Dialectic.
The Church disowned, the tower overthrown, the bells up-
    turned, what have we to do
But stand with empty hands and palms turned upwards
In an age which advances progressively backwards?

Thomas Stearns Eliot, 1888-1965. From THE ROCK

[121]

PRAYER FROM THE BRINK

Give us faces of stone
To set against the drift,
To set against the swift, strong, headlong
Currents swollen to a torrent
That is sweeping our world away.
We are of the Rock
(Give us faces of stone!)
But if the Rock crumble to pebbles
Then pebbles and all the whitened water
Swirl unchecked to the fathomless deeps
Where Thy Day is never seen.

Give us wills of steel
And be our magnetic pole.
Draw us unwavering through the wastes
Whence the signs of salvation are vanishing.
Thou art our journey's end
(Give us wills of steel!)
The World has forgotten its Home
And the things that belong to its Peace.
If our compass fail
Our footsteps stagger and reel
And all our marchings nothing avail
But to bring us back on ourselves in circles,
In dizzying, nightmare, maniac rings
From whence is no release.
Draw us home.

Give us hearts of flame
To burn against the cold
To burn against the old, the mortal chill
The quenching thrill
Of the fast-flooding tide.
Thou art Fire and Light
(Give us hearts of flame!)

Make us to burn like beacons
In defiance of ancient Night.
Make us braziers in the cold streets of the cities,
Make us lamps in Thy sanctuaries,
Make us candles to the Sacred Heart.
The World is lost, and is looking for the Way.

M. Farrow

NIGHT THOUGHTS

I woke up with foreboding, and despair
Lurked in the gloomy shadows of the night;
But very weak and foolish is my care
  If Jesus Christ was right.

All the grim puzzles of the universe
Compassed me round, all Nature's endless fight;
But I shall see a blessing, not a curse,
  If Jesus Christ was right.

And most of all, longing for those who died
Smote at my heart with overwhelming might;
But I shall see them and be satisfied
  If Jesus Christ was right.

Lord, unto Thee in the old words I cry,
'Illumine my dark spirit with Thy light.'
Oh save me from the sin of accidie,
  And let me know Thee right.

H. C. Bradby, 1868-1947

CHRISTMAS

The bells of waiting Advent ring,
   The Tortoise stove is lit again
And lamp-oil light across the night
   Has caught the streaks of winter rain
In many a stained-glass window sheen
From Crimson Lake to Hooker's Green.

The holly in the windy hedge
   And round the Manor House the yew
Will soon be stripped to deck the ledge,
   The altar, font and arch and pew,
So that the villagers can say
'The church looks nice' on Christmas Day.

Provincial public houses blaze
   And Corporation tramcars clang.
On lighted tenements I gaze
   Where paper decorations hang,
And bunting in the red Town Hall
Says 'Merry Christmas to you all.'

And London shops on Christmas Eve
   Are strung with silver bells and flowers
As hurrying clerks the City leave
   To pigeon-haunted classic towers,
And marbled clouds go scudding by
The many-steepled London sky.

And girls in slacks remember Dad,
   And oafish louts remember Mum,
And sleepless children's hearts are glad,
   And Christmas-morning bells say 'Come!'
Even to shining ones who dwell
Safe in the Dorchester Hotel.

And is it true? And is it true,
   This most tremendous tale of all,
Seen in a stained-glass window's hue,
   A Baby in an ox's stall?
The Maker of the stars and sea
Become a child on earth for me?

And is it true? For if it is,
   No loving fingers tying strings
Around those tissued fripperies,
   The sweet and silly Christmas things,
Bath salts and inexpensive scent
And hideous tie so kindly meant,

No love that in a family dwells,
   No carolling in frosty air,
Nor all the steeple-shaking bells
   Can with this single Truth compare—
That God was Man in Palestine
And lives today in Bread and Wine.

John Betjeman, 1906-